Zenku 365

OTHER BOOKS BY JAY VERNEY

POETRY

*The Mindful Art of Verandaku: Micro Poems in a Macro
World – Volume 1*
*The Mindful Art of Verandaku: Micro Poems in a Macro
World – Volume 2*

FICTION

A Mortality Tale
Percussion
Spawned Secrets
Summon Up The Blood

MEMOIR

*The Women Come & Go and The Women Came & Went:
A Memoir & An Essay*

NON-FICTION

*Creating A Custom Fit In An Off-The-Rack Genre World:
The Proximal Investigator, The Corpse of Convenience,
and Their Family of Circumstance in Crime Fiction*

Zenku 365

A Zenku A Day
Invites Mindfulness
To Stay

禅句

Jay Verney

ZEN KETTLE BOOKS | BRISBANE, QLD

Zen Kettle Books

Email: steaming@zenkettle.com
www.zenkettle.com

Publisher's Note: This is a work of poetry and non-fiction. Names, characters, places, and incidents may be a product of the author's imagination. Locales and public names are sometimes used for atmospheric purposes. Any resemblance to actual people, living or dead, or to businesses, companies, events, institutions, or locales is completely coincidental.

Book Cover Design: © Zen Kettle Design at zenkettle.com
Cover Image: © 2016 by VernLaw Images.
Other Images: © VernLaw Images
Book Layout © 2015 BookDesignTemplates.com

National Library of Australia Cataloguing-in-Publication entry

Author: Verney, Jay.
Title: Zenku 365 – A Zenku A Day Invites Mindfulness To Stay
Subjects: Poetry.
             Poetry, Modern—21st century.

Dewey No: A821.4

ISBN 978-0-9945470-4-0

TABLE OF CONTENTS

AUTHOR NOTE

Zenku 365 was a New Year's resolution that stuck. My blog, Zen Kettle (at zenkettle.wordpress.com), features Zenkus on all kinds of subjects and they're published every few days. Who knows, they could go on forever like that, or at least until I'm fitted for a wooden overcoat. But I also wanted to create an additional and self-contained Zenku project and this book is the result.

Zenku is the sister of Verandaku (yes, indeed, there are siblings, and Verandaku has a blog, Veranda Life, at www.verandalife.com, and a two-volume series in paperback and ebook formats). Both are the daughters of Haiku, the Japanese poetic form read and written around the world.

Zenkus are my take on free-form micro poems without the constraint of the traditional 5-7-5 syllable three-line structure of the Haiku (and Verandaku). Read on to embrace Zenkus for fun, laughs, pleasure and leisure.

For Momo

Zenku? What's A Zenku?

Zenku: the art
of
moments

Jay Verney

WHAT
All and
no
thing

HOW
Sound and body
Mind and heart
Dark matter Light

WHEN
Without notice
With attention
With love

WHERE
Here and here
There there there
Every momentary where

WHY
Moments are how
we live
Zenku them, grasshopper

WHO
You
Me
Us

Jay Verney

Zenku

1 – 365
Plus a Leap Zenku
Plus Spares, Just Because
Plus A Micro Workshop

1

Resolution day

the first

of many

2

Seconds take many

forms and time – just

desserts, melting moments

3

Sitting quietly

welcoming the

breath

4

The sea breeze

arriving late

Waves on strike?

5

Do small apples

keep small

doctors away?

6

How do you

remember rain?

Spits, showers, storms?

7

Wednesday's child is

full of

mid-week malaise

8

Pot of tea

Bringer of steamy

depths

9

The paperweight

heavying a

light read

10

Kittens growling

at each other

Growth spurting

11

Ordinary hours

offering

extraordinary minutes

12

My cat's first

birthday

calculated in purrs

13

Raisin toast hot

butter-worthy

Bite it, bite

14

On Google streetview

my childhood home

We're long gone

15

The washing dried

and folded

sun warmth built in

16

Excluding the tail

swish a

dozing kitten

17

Hanging raindrops

meet their fate

Windy assassin

18

Down the roadworks

road

walking

19

At twilight

a dog's silhouette

loping

20

Beneath the

thickening poinciana

shade and ... shade

21

Sun shower

cloud shower

Raindrop tribes

22

Clouds travel in

gangs storming

the sky

23

Pineapple flummery made

by a You Tube stranger

Almost exactly Mum's

24

Cats stretched flat

and sleeping – long

narrow, funny carpets

25

A week between

the Sunday papers

and fresh scandals

26

Walking past Meals

on Wheels smelling

lunch at breakfast

27

Too many steps

in pinchy shoes

So run

28

Roadworks inching

closer a

tractor-feed street

29

A friend's

half-century wholly

lived

30

Up the down

hill steeper than

I remember

31

On election day

opposites attracted to

the ballot box

32

Where chickens once

escaped birdbrain

bamboozling battens

33

Wednesday's surprises on

a two day delay

reading Monday's mail

34

Rain drenched tree

wind-shaken makes

a sun shower

35

New filing cabinet

steely weight outside

paper-light within

36

As I meditate

a cat pads by

strolling mindfully

37

Ground sodden

Humidity high

Sunday

38

At noon a

trip to the mailbox

Empty but for heat

39

Showers in waves

sunlit and clouded

Colour to greyscale

40

The fan blowing

cold at 3 a.m.

Blanket or switch?

41

Stars from childhood

waiting patiently for

 my gazing return

42

Rotting mangoes

turning but still

Microbial magic

43

Second slice of

cheesecake, delight

declining, but slowly

44

Friend leaving early

Aftershave lingering

Dinner ghost

45

Mud farming wasp

as busy as a

bee

46

Slice of apple

from my love

The sweeter hands

47

Fan squeaking on

a hot night

Every other dream

48

Old pegs

past it

Clothesline cling-ons

49

On his motorbike

arms outstretched

Welcoming speed

50

Old socks

drooping and thin

softly comforting

51

Tropical storm

along the coast

Hot *and* bothering

52

Walking through a

newly mown lawn

Soles greening grassily

53

Local pier

the beach's

long veranda

54

New curls on

an old vine

Paler imitations

55

Turf squares:

grassy tiles

dirty glue

56

Waiting for the

heat to break

Sweating up a storm

57

Singing birds

at midnight

Yesterday today tomorrow

58

A light fog

A light breakfast

Mist and tea

59

Racing bikes

whir by

speed-blending air

60

Many noises to

count at 3 a.m.

instead of sheep

お茶
TEA

Zenku 365 #58

61

Stocky guy stocky

dog waddling

each other home

62

Gardening golfer

weed whacking with

his nine iron

63

Barometer falling

Ant hills rising

Humans hoarding

64

Summer heat in

autumn

A lathering legacy

65

Birds watch us walk

and fly off

shrieking with laughter

66

The neighbour's party

Music in need of

a power failure

67

Kittens welcomed home

Life in gecko

fast lane begins

68

It was sudden

explosive and satisfying:

the sneeze

69

Weed shadows as

sharp and delicate

as flowers

70

Butcherbird fluttering

with a snack

Grass, fence, branch

71

New homes and old

Old lawns and new

The same sun

72

Peeling-paint windows

offer their fresh

daily views

73

Our walking shadows

separating merging

Colour blind

74

In my mechanic's

office a display of

toy cars, engineless

75

Straighter than arrows

road feels longer

than its winding mate

76

Sacrificial water wine

bread milk and beer

Dyed for St Patrick

77

A midnight chorus line

of wanton emptiness:

taxi row waiting

78

Messy doona cloud

off to the south

Blue sheets due north

79

Green waste collector

on his day off

plays the blues

80

Truckload of palettes

loadless and stacked

Sleeper shift

81

Glassed water

tapped and running

only seconds ago

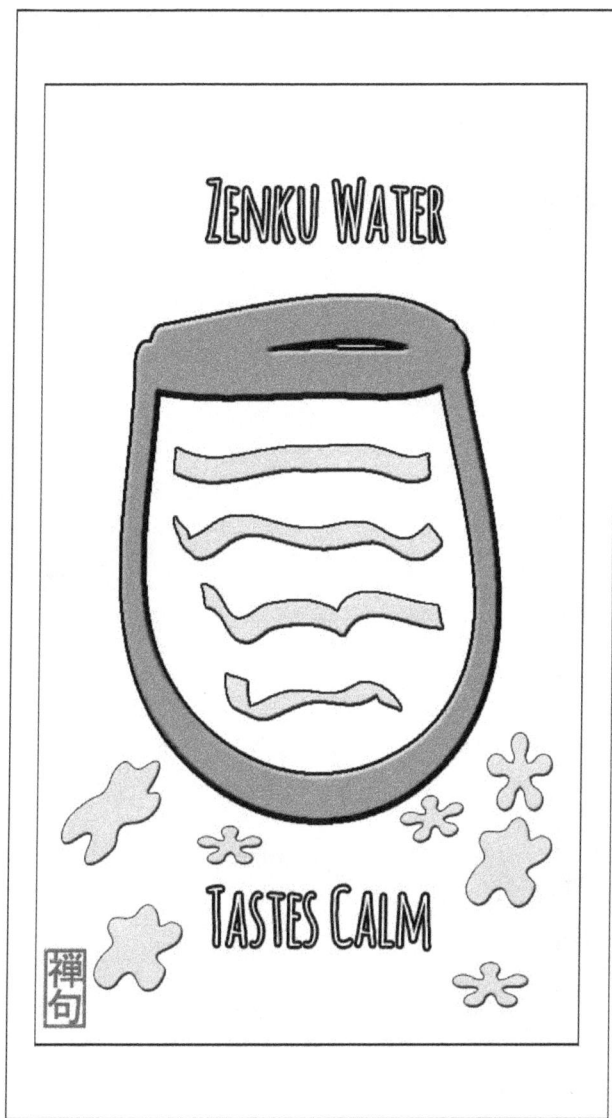

Zenku 365 #81

82

Do not live to

fit in be

fit to live in

83

The 6 a.m. smog

of a million

smokers gasping

84

In darkness thunder

rolling through showers

of thoughts

85

Calling from the cyclone

zone my cousin

brings an air rush

86

No need to speak

so loudly now

the roof drum's softened

87

On the veranda

kittens' fur damp

with storm spray

88

Typing them out

the sound of

each letter inky

89

The kitten asleep

along my arm

heavier with each breath

90

The sun gone

for days – night time

not so dark

91

Capturing moments

word by phrase

threaded lines of praise

92

Pegging the washing

out each load

an anthology

93

Today's chicken lunch

olive oil, garlic, tomato

Sourdough chew and crunch

94

Strolling beneath a

poinciana's breezy shower

Yesterday's raindrops

95

Newly trimmed hedge

Flat top level

Curls gone to ground

96

Up-the-hill leg

muscles with

downhill aspirations

97

Word and sentence

lullabies from a

silent, inky instrument

98

Meditating with kittens

teaching me

dust mote-ology

99

Zimmerframe traffic jam

at the café

Nanas cruising brunch

100

Watching a kitten's

tail telling

mood-swing tales

101

Cloud banks rising

above each other

Their windy fates

102

Grassy blades drift by

after the mowing

Proof of lawn

103

Leftover washer after

the build – special

or extra special

104

Thunderheads reaching for

the sun playing

rise and shine

105

After his death

the empty bed

full of impressions

Zenku 365 #105

106

If your pets wait

for you after life

do they speak?

107

Tan dog's owner in

a tan shirt the

solidarity of chance

108

Disorders of toadstools

overnighting on a

grassy campground

109

Black and white dogs

Black and white birds

watch their green yard mown

110

How many drops

in a shower

there must be

111

Thinking of my dead

brother I speak

in his style

112

Waiting all day for

the forecast rain

Slept through it

113

Rain heavy and

light reaching the ground

loudly and softer

114

Storm clouds following

their cool change

envoy

115

Carrying a letter

to a friend

Its' weightless love

116

Lizards race my rake

through autumn's leaves

winning by a rustle

117

Breakfast storm

The garden clatters

with rain

118

Laughing so hard

I forget why but

the aching knows

119

Toads at twilight

scarier than

toads at dawn

120

Mist sifting through

hilltops inviting it

to rest

121

Up in the sky

a bird a plane

no super man

122

Schoolkids all over the

park like ants

on sugared lettuce

123

Autumn blue sky

horizon to horizon

Accessory free

124

Young cyclist freewheeling

Old cyclist braking

Hill of all ages

125

Carload of pupils

driving to exams

A study on wheels

126

Clouds sketched on

with the wispiest

pencil – atmospheric afterthought

127

Kittens leaping yards

as the crow flies

Slightly uneven contest

128

Do a few short

minutes equal

several long ones?

129

Does a quick

stop here equal

morning tea there?

130

Learning of a

death weeks past

Grief ready and waiting

131

Sock poised on the

laundry basket's lip

Gravity courting trouble

132

Fallen limbs gather for

a sub-branch meeting

United we stood

133

Noisy airplane engine

silencing the magic

of flight

134

Late morning fog

steaming home

at a leisurely pace

135

Clouds flattening

against the sky

like ironed sheets

136

Pawprints and shoeprints

tattoo a concrete path

Who stepped first?

137

Sunny, still, blue

sky day, and mild

Resale value zero

138

Rainbow lorikeets breakfasting

on yellow, munching

through the spectrum

139

Black and white

Black and white

Fly-by magpie

140

Too few words too

many

Singles and herds of them

141

Two days missing

from my diary

Discounted year

142

Crow descending on

a windless day

Unflappable

143

Boney frame awaiting

hat, shirt and coat

New house

144

Discarded plastic spoon

Evidence of foam

Stirring frothy memories

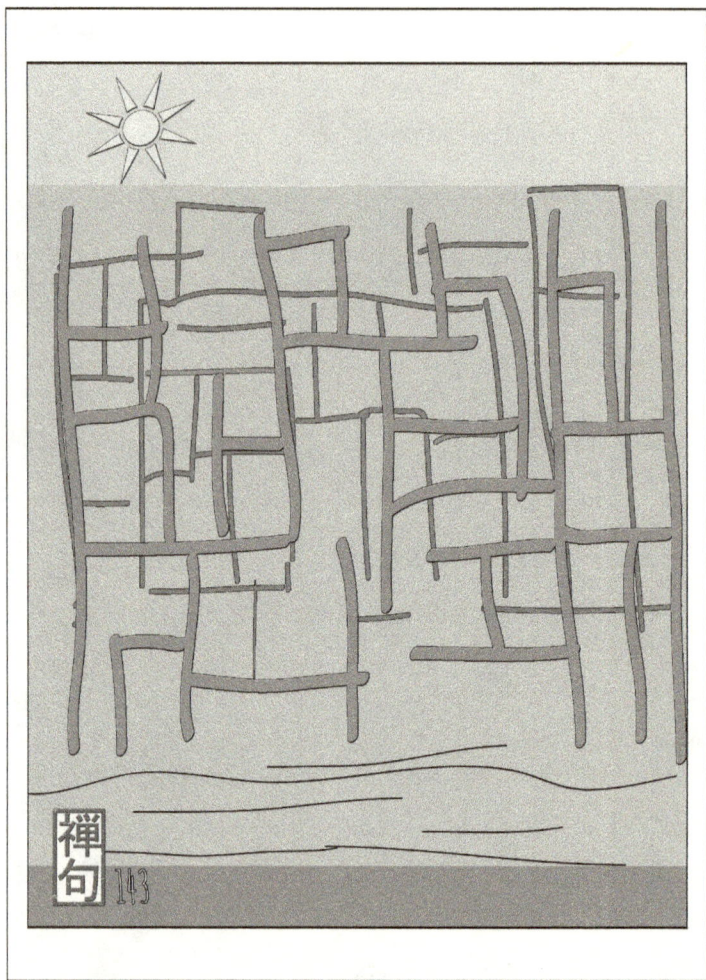

Zenku 365 #143

145

Red ball flying

Black dog leaping

Green grass softens

146

Yorkie nosing footpath

sleuthing freedom's scent

Hobbyist at best

147

Clouds spreading like

a shaken peacock's

plumage – sky fright

148

Bamboo shoots above

the treeline

Spindly ambition

149

Empty house for rent

its yard full

of nature's tenants

150

Shrubs and creepers grow

through their fences

Enticing compliments

151

Birds' wings flapping

so closely I

think I'm flying

152

Closed doors and

windows steaming

kettle winter's come

153

Walking too fast

to notice I'm

walking too fast

Zenku 365 #152

154

My warm cat on

my warm lap

A winter friendship

155

Sun rising behind

stripes of cloud

A Venetian dawn

156

Beneath frangipani beside

wild rosemary scented

moments breezing

157

Long after the fire

pink camellias blooming

through the kitchen floor

158

House sold – empty

Pool moss – greening

Herb garden – drying

159

A jet's vapour trail

wind-twisted a bending

white tree branch

160

Upside-down thunderheads

tickling the treeline

with wispy mist

161

Through train windows

commuter silhouettes

Dozing reading watching

162

Walking this street again

after months

The old dogs gone

163

At the piano student's

house scales and

arpeggios with breakfast

164

Boiled eggs pianissimo

Kettle steamily whistling

Musical moving treats

165

Late morning walk more

traffic more dust the

bloom off dawn's rose

166

Tear trails tracing

windscreens after

a dewy night

167

Tractor mower guy wool

beanie steely-eyed blades

sharp grass lying low

168

Today's checklist written

Play with kittens

Check

169

Every step gripping

grass dirt path

Banking earthy capital

170

Coldest day so far

Chilling reminders drill

my autumn sleeves

171

On the top step

a Buddha

Enlightenment at the door

Jay Verney

172

Cheering winter's solstice

on its way

Heat and light

173

A white sun

mooning behind

thinning fog

174

Full moon behind

Full sun ahead

Today's sky between

175

Empty red car

Empty yellow trailer

Moving day blues

176

Weeds reaching for

the sky like thin

startled cowboys – hatless

177

On the horizon

showers water-colouring a

red and blue dusk

178

Kids playing ball games

Rules as rubbery as

arms and legs

179

Cyclists' steaming backs

The rising sun's

first heat

180

Half-grown magpie

feathers thickening

bird-song lengthening

181

Storm-homeless worms

searching for

slitherworthy digs

182

Muddy footprints enjoy

temporary immortality – the

sun's dry wit

183

Tree-seeping mist

Street-muffling fog

Mild winter day

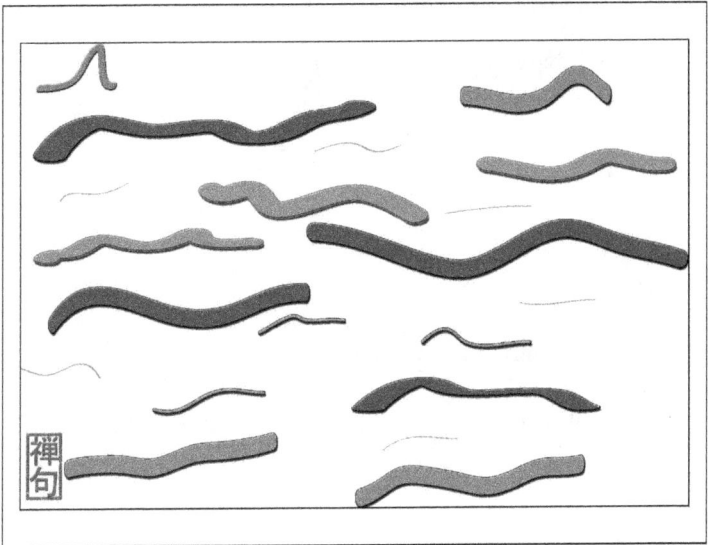

Zenku 365 #181

184

Hilltop sun, fog-bound

gully – don't go for

wispy in-between

185

Palm fronds flapping

like birds' wings –

manifestly grounded

186

Rosella flock in

from the west

Drought breaking habits

187

Purple door on

an old house

Visitors tickled pink

188

Cloud trails cross

high up – X marks

the temporary spot

189

Newly mown grass

fresher than

a moment

190

Street roaming ibis

Gravity pressed wing

Takeoff feathering closer

191

Sometimes the sun

helps clouds look

stormy – sometimes they are

192

A lone crow in

a lone tree

Happy couple

193

The spacious silence

of intersections

after traffic

194

The odd spit

from way up

Bored clouds playing

195

Fog roll below

the tree line

Lingering spare tyre

196

Winter walking warmth

arrives – sleeve roll

finger stretch – aaahh

197

New houses

almost finished

Stories to come

198

Morning walk

Running late

Jogging home – not

199

Newly dug garden

Worms arrive with

dirty baggage

200

Hearing my footsteps

I remember

I am here

201 – Irregular Verb

Rivers will run

Taps can run

I don't run

202

Magpies landscape the

garden with

their latest songs

203

Walking a path

older than hills

Raindrops footsteps petals

204

Clouds dabbed piecemeal

onto the blue

Bunching, trailing glue, sagging

205

Framed and surging

between power poles

Full moon

206

8 a.m. sun floodlighting

storm clouds

Beyond a mellow drama

207

My childhood pencil

case – old lead

new pages

208 – Porridge Suite #1

After the *MasterChef*

finale a bowl of

porridge – milk honey

208 – Porridge Suite #2

After the *MasterChef*

finale a bowl of

porridge – no honey

208 – Porrdige Suite #3

After the *MasterChef*

finale

a bowl

稀飯
PORRIDGE

Zenku 365 #208

209

Outside the café

speed-reading the news

Winter frost

210

Taking a fallen branch

for a snake we

move faster than kids

211

A following dog

not mine

Loaner pet

212

That deepest breath

to lung's bottom

The living end

213

On moonless nights

my torch paltry

and powerful

214

Thinking I would

travel the world

I began walking

215

The wallphone

in the kitchen

Immobile

216

Saw a morning

rainbow perfectly natural

naturally perfect art

217

Showers windily

discombobulated

barely touch down

218

Dandelions everywhere

Weeds growing like –

weeds

219

Mist lifting steamily

with the sun's

morning fry-up

220

Shady trees

openly sunning

themselves

221

The sun

seeking solace

found cloudy relief

222

Empty football field

Magpies grub-hunting

the divots

223

No sign of

the Lollipop Lady

She's signing in

224

Umbrellas unfurling

and furling rainy

spitty sunny lives

225

Seconds arrive

and depart

Moments bare all

226

Paws tucked under

Eyes half-almonds

Kitten becoming cat

227

Butcher bird swooping

breakfast under the

crow's ravenous stare

228

Clouds arcing like

three-quarter rainbows

Colourless imitations

229

Empty park bench

plenty of thinking

room

230

Two-tone hills

shades of

sun and cloud

231

Repairing the road

less travelled

for the few

232

Before they move

house their winter

garden rose blooms

233

Four rainbow lorikeets

flying their colours

in chattering formation

234

Dog and man

running leashed to

each other's rhythm

235

Same lunch same

place same time

Consistent? Safe? Circadian

236

Cat stretches lengthily

Paws claim my

foot, gently – at first

237 – 3 a.m. Suite #1

Refrigerator humming

Wall clock ticking

3 a.m. friends

237 – 3 a.m. Suite #2

Fridge humming

Wall clock ticking

3 a.m. comfort

237 – 3 a.m. Suite #3

Fridge humming

Wall clock ticking

3 a.m. duet

238

Trees emerging unscathed

from early fog

Their dripping shapeliness

239

Valley fog like

whipped cream – skim

milk higher up

Zenku 365 #237

240

Chewing her nails

Grooming the rough

edges before cat napping

241

Inland birds

at the shore

Drought pushing boundaries

242

Following the moon

it follows me

home

243

On my walk, the

same old trees

showing off Spring

244

The new sofa

barely sat upon

Its precise cushions

245

Cooking salmon for

the first time –

sorry, little fish

246

The cat purring

The clock ticking

The kettle boils

247

Surrounded by books

Pages unturned tonight

Tired eyes, tired

248

Two plus five plus

seven crows a

murderous dozen plus change

249

Hungry spider on

the shortcut footpath

Mind your feet

250

Ambulance shriek nearing

Traffic huddles

sidelong

251

Garden daisies face

to face embedding

a petal friendship

252

Gusting wind

Watering eyes

Go inside

253

Kittens grooming each

other only sometimes

biting ears

254

Crows breakfasting on

the front lawn –

fearless hunger

255

Sun resistant

morning smog a

breeze to remove

256

Cold front gusting

at closed windows

Glassy-eyed rebuff

257

Leafless winter tree

just a gang

of big twigs

258

Blithering jibber-jabber

step after step

Monkey, no, human mind

259

Clouds doubling and

doubling before

gusty vandals swoop

260

Five-dollar note and

a dead noisy miner on

today's walking paths

261

Dead noisy miner

as silent as

the lowest clouds

262

Dead noisy miner

wings neatly tucked

Beak mid-note

263

Empty veranda hammock

still swinging

Unexpected door knock

264

Moth to the

bright lamp – cat

to the drab moth

265

Pen cap lost

Words fading

letter by letter

266

Two old dogs

lolloping together all

the world's time

267

Cat's shiny plate

after raw mince

cleaner than clean

268

Big pawed cat

quite small in

the grand scheme

269

Every morning the

dawn light and

crows, clearing their throats

270

Plodders strollers walkers

shufflers joggers runners

Ambulatory caste system

271

Breathing life into

a fridge-chilled bug

It flies away

272

Little traffic jams

on quiet streets

Morning rush minute

273

Rain spitting like a

timid audience clapping

Hesitant at first

274

Dog trio one walker

the sound of

three leads plaiting

275

Stepping through autumn's

last leafy offspring

Fifty shades of brown

276

Morning mist sitting

on the hills like

First Communion veils

277

Left sneaker right thong*

side by side

near the playground

(*Thongs in Australia are flip-flops elsewhere)

278

Dead fan's blades

spinning on

the windy footpath

279

New coats for

all seasons

Painting fences

280

Thin mist barely

earning its name

Gone in blinks

281

Summer makes an

early run on Spring

Caught long-sleeved

282

Walking between

a crow and

its shadow

283

Leaves unraked

relax in their

midday falling pattern

284

Rain, spotting the

ground, begins

to fall

285

Late blooming jacarandas

worrying the lavender

out of us

286

Tuesday after a

long weekend work

almost an after thought

287

This new kitten

asleep on my lap

An old hand

288

Cyclist free-wheels

Parrot down-drafts

Meeting at hill's bottom

289

Red chopper in a

blue and white sky

French air space

290

Phone left

at home

Messages immobilised

291

On the library's wi-fi'd

garden, Skyping across countries

and seasons

292

Bevelled and tinted

this shade and that

Storm clouds sunning themselves

293

Birdsong, bicycle bell

Toddler chatter, toast crunch

Morning chorus lines

294

Thousands of miles

on these soles

Barely begun

295

Fallen jacaranda leaves

twitching a

breezey farewell

296

Running late

Joining the queue

Early now

Jay Verney

297

Waiting for the

bus train ferry

Walking to work waiting

298

Boarding the ferry

morning and evening

Waving to work and home

299

Commuters on platform soles

on platform one

Layer upon layer

Zenku 365 #298

300

The bus packed like

sardines – no oil

baguette or pepper

301

Sunny cloudy sunny

cloudy day a

stone-washed denim sky

302

Fresh leaves boiling in

our new old pot

Second-hand seasoning

303

The same breakfast

each different dawn

Unvarying comfort

304

Visitors lure out

every corner's dust

motes, no exceptions

305

Electrical storm lightening

the night sky

lightning fast

306

Thunder rolling by

the kitten at my side

comfortably fearful

307

The hedge

just clipped

A seasonal geometry

308

A man and

his dog love

on a leash

309

Openly shady

trees

Arboreal intent

310

Jasmine Spring

jasmine leaves

jasmine tea

311

Auctioned house with

a vacant stare

Draw the curtains

312

All day thundery

showery cloudy skies

Nothing decisive

313

On the long

chase lorikeets

slip-streaming each other

314

New mulch around

old trees not

quite perfect circles

315

Soldiers generally

Generals specifically

Heroes particularly

316

Bamboo waving

above tree tops

Dozing energy

317

Tangle of garden

worms an apprentice

Gorgon's starter hair

318

Rain clouds lowering

themselves for a

showery tickle

319

Dry air on my

face heat gusting

from an arid centre

320

After the flat

tarmac, soft grass

The homeliness

321

Crossing the street for

a bush full of

blooming roses – cerise

322

Sixty years tamed a

garden newly wild its

keeper with the earth

323

Turn off the light

Turn on the shade

Cool down

324

Thunder every so

often summer's surge

degrees away

325

Rain's smell

The hum of

rooftops cooling

326

Swept floor open

windows gusty dusty

day unswept floor

327

Humidity high

Energy flat a

kites and pancakes day

328

Quiet day

feeling okay

No need to pray

329

Waving my beloved

off to work

A slow departure

330

House removalists take two

and a half

Half the memories left

331

The building site

mixing

voices and cement

332

The cats

welcome me home

with clawed purrs

333

Spindles of pine

rising above

mayhems of shrubbery

334

The sky's summer

showers sweating on

a new day

335

Chairs line the

wall awaiting a

table dance

Zenku 365 #335

336

House removal truck

idling – the house

standing its ground

337

White milk jug on

the breakfast table

Liquid white in solid

338

Ginger-haired man

Ginger-furred spaniel

Their black leash

339

Green parrots gossip

daylight out of

the darkness

340

Soles dark as

topsoil decades

gardening shoeless

341

A little shower as

we meet our friends

Raindrops with breakfast

342

Raining over there

keeping to itself

Skirting the sun

343

New pianist next

door scaling octaves

with minor success

344

Imagine the sound

of paint drying

(Better than watching, surely)

345

Walking by a

ground-settled magpie

singing up breakfast

346

Small birds chatter

Big birds flee

Slow scaredy crows

347

Black white fuzzy brown

Mother and fledgling

magpies inseparable diners

348

Leaves laughing themselves

loose

in the wind

349

After the house

removal its lawn

plants a grassover

350

Seatless bike leans

against a lamp post

Only standing room

351

After midnight's storm

cool fresh air

A wakeful stillness

352

Crows tormenting dusk

with their tuneless

one-note songs

353

Fairy lights reflecting

generously from every

shiny surface

354

Cats groom their

slender legs with the

tongue-strokes of artists

355

Shelved books

Covers closed

Stories in for the night

356

On summer solstice

night twilight

dilly-dallying

357

Hundreds of corellas

screech the day awake

Dawn's silence distant

358

Pencils pointedly

colouring page

upon page

359

Dessert on Christmas

Day a

trifling matter

360

The cracked cup

full of memories

doesn't leak

361

Sidelong glances from

hungry crows at

my empty hands

362

The branch falling

a metre ahead

Blatant *memento mori*

363

The branch falls

a metre behind

Memento mori playful

364

On the long road

short steps each one

its own destination

365

Last moment on

the last day

Anticipating

Plus a Leap Zenku 366

Warm air on my

face fresh currents

from a tropical space

And a Spare, just because

Fog's paltriness

beneath a risen

sun

And Another, for fun

Trees shrubs ferns grass

hogging

the green

Zenku Workshop
How to Zenku A Moment (or Two)

This workshop follows two Zenkus as they're created, from first observations and thoughts to the final few words and three lines. The first one is about some towels I saw hanging on a line when I was out walking one summer's day.

Workshop Zenku One

- Towels on the line in a back yard
- They look like beach towels
- They're out there to dry

Those thoughts are in the front of your mind in nano-seconds. You might choose to ignore them, or to take them further down the path of a Zenku moment.

So, 'Towels on the line in a back yard,' becomes:
- Towels line dry

That's all you need to suggest an image.

Then, 'They look like beach towels,' becomes:
- after the beach

following on from line one, and that's all you need to suggest all kinds of beachy images and memories.

Finally, 'They're out there to dry,' has been taken care of in our new line one. So now we can consider a punch line which will shift focus to what's really going on there on the clothes line. The wind, along with the sunshine, is drying the towels. They'll twirl around and shake out some loose sand if they've simply been pegged up to dry out because, who knows, the owners might be going back to the beach again today. All of which leads to:

- Sand-shifting wind

This would be sufficient to complete the Zenku, but to further suggest more about the nature of sand in fabric and the effects of wind and gravity, we can change a word and our line will read:

- Sand-sifting wind

The word 'sift' is suggestive of grains of sand falling, rolling, blowing out onto the grass or into the air as the towels hang around. And if you remove the hyphen between the first two words, both sand and wind can own the sifting, but that's optional.

The final product, moving from 18 words to 9 (or 20 syllables to 12:

Towels line dry

after the beach

Sand-sifting wind

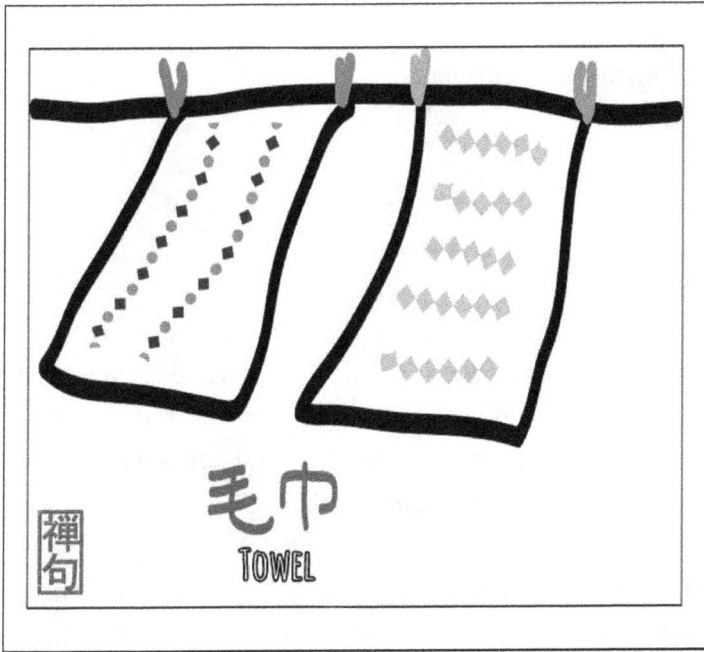

毛巾
TOWEL

禅句

Workshop Zenku Two

This second zenku, coincidentally, also involves a clothes line, but in this case, it's confined to the pegs and it references *Star Trek* (just a warning, in case you're either a big *Star Trek* fan, or not so much of one).

First thoughts arrived in this form:
- Old pegs past their
- prime on the line
- Still clinging tighter

Which then morphed into:
- Old clothes pegs past their
- prime still on the line
- clinging tightly

I'd added a word. Yikes! I wasn't sure that everyone would realise I meant clothes pegs when I wrote pegs, though that's probably a given. Nonetheless, I added clothes, moved 'still' around, and changed 'tighter' to 'tightly.'

But this is far too long for my liking. So, if the pegs are past their prime, then the word 'old' becomes redundant. And if they're on the line, well, they're on the line, so 'still' can be given the heave-ho, until:
- Clothes pegs past their prime
- on the line
- clinging tightly

Using some less formal, more everyday speech we can tidy up lines one and three:

- Clothes pegs past it
- on the line
- Clinging on

The last two words of the poem remind me of the famous and notorious Klingons from *Star Trek,* which encourages a teaspoon of fun:

- Clothes pegs past
- it on the line
- Cling-ons

Done and dusted, unless you want to reinstate 'old' in the interests of emphasis and not being ageist – plenty of old pegs carry on carrying their laundry loads well beyond expectations. Plus, we achieve a further reduction in wordage from 11 to 6 words (or 13 syllables to 8):

Old pegs

past it

Clothesline cling-ons

There it is,then, a brief tutorial on Zenku moments. I hope you enjoyed it, and that it will be of some use to you as you capture your own observations and create your precious Zenkus. Happy coaxing, dear reader, and thank you so much for reading.

About the Author

Jay Verney is an Australian author who has published novels, essays, short stories, poetry, memoir, magazine and newspaper columns, book and film reviews, and comics.

Jay's first novel, *A Mortality Tale,* was shortlisted for the Australian/*Vogel* and Miles Franklin Literary Awards (and is available as both a paperback and an ebook). Jay has a PhD (in genre and crime fiction), and a Master's degree (memoir) in Creative Writing from the University of Queensland. In

2009, she received a Dean's Award for Outstanding Research Higher Degree Thesis for her PhD.

Jay's second novel, *Percussion*, is available in both ebook and paperback, as is her third novel, *Spawned Secrets*. Her fourth novel, *Summon Up The Blood*, is a result of her PhD and is also a paperback and an ebook, along with the essay that accompanied the novel, *Creating A Custom Fit In An Off-The-Rack Genre World.* Jay's memoir, *The Women Come & Go* includes an essay, *The Women Came & Went,* a reflection on writing the memoir and how writers research and re-imagine history and lives. It's available in, wait for it, paperback and ebook formats, too. Celebrate. Volumes One and Two of *The Mindful Art of Verandaku* are waiting mindfully for you as ebooks and paperbacks. Very nice.

Visit virtual Jay at her websites for **free** entertainment:

Transient Total Focus – www.jayverney.net
One blink at a time
The mother ship, where minty fresh stuff and nonsense and even some useful things reside.

Veranda Life – www.verandalife.com
Breathe ~ Relax ~Drink Black Tea Often
999 lovely haikus with lovely images, and the inspiration for this book. All the images are there, too. Enjoy.

Zen Kettle – www.zenkettle.wordpress.com
It makes tea

Zenkus, teeny tiny haikus about life, the universe, and everything. Also lovely.

Last Cat On Mars – www.lastcatonmars.wordpress.com
Would you want to be the first?
Dr On Mars welcomes you to a comical world of fun and laughs. It's laughly, and lovely, yes.

You can give Jay all your money by visiting Amazon to purchase even more of her darling works. Ask Prof. Google for 'Jay Verney Amazon.' You know you want to, grasshopper.

If you enjoyed this book, please don't hesitate to *visit Amazon and post a review*. The author will be so grateful, she'll send you a picture of your very own avatar in minifigure world posing with the Martially famous Last Cat On Mars and also, a bonus flamington (fake lamington, but you knew that) and naturally the blessings of her father's very loud motorbike, *La Banshee*.

Acknowledgements

As usual, Lorrie has been more than generous and supportive
of this project, casting a wise and critical eye over
proceedings, and ensuring that every cat, human and feline,
cool dude and warmly furry, was loved and nurtured with tea
and scones, mince and kibble. That kibble, tastes good.
Mmmm....

Clouds rising
with the sun
A breakfast spread

www.ingramcontent.com/pod-product-compliance
Lightning Source LLC
Chambersburg PA
CBHW031549040426
42452CB00006B/248

9780994547040